# SCIENCE SKILLS 4

# 1 HOW DO OUR BODY SYSTEMS WORK?

## 1 Match to make correct sentences.

**a** Body systems are

**b** The locomotor system

**c** The nervous system

**d** The digestive system

**e** The excretory system

○ extracts nutrients from the food we eat.

○ helps eliminate waste from the body.

○ allows us to move around.

○ groups of organs that work together to perform a specific task.

○ controls our body, allowing the different parts of it to communicate.

## 2 Identify the body systems and write their names.

**a**

_____

_____

**b**

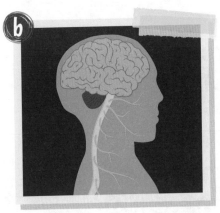

_____

_____

**c**

_____

_____

2

**3 Label the diagram of the respiratory system.**

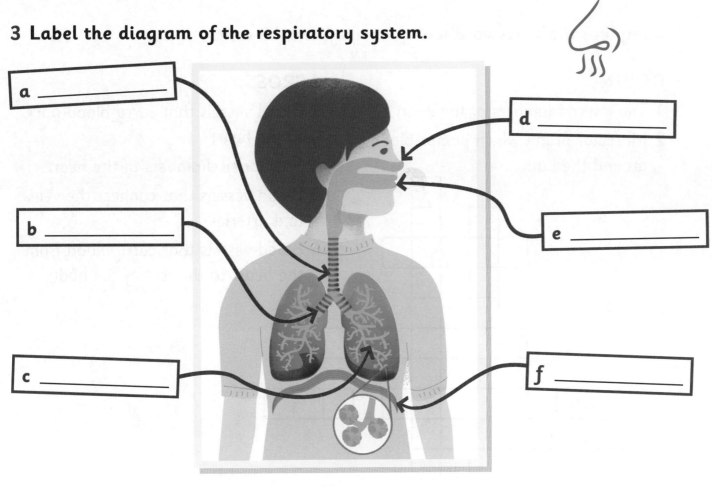

a _____

b _____

c _____

d _____

e _____

f _____

**4 Complete the sentences to describe respiration.**

bronchi   drawn   expelled   lungs   mouth   nose   tube

**a** Air enters our body through the _____ and the _____ .

**b** The air passes through a _____ called the trachea.

**c** The _____ are at the end of the trachea, and lead to the _____ .

**d** When the diaphragm contracts, air is _____ into our lungs.

**e** When the diaphragm relaxes, air is _____ from our lungs.

**5 Read the description and write the word on the line.**

**a** These smaller tubes are found at the end of the bronchi.               _____

**b** The alveoli are covered in these.               _____

**c** These are tiny air sacs found at the end of each bronchiole.               _____

## 6 Complete the crossword using words from the unit.

**DOWN**

1 The lower chambers of the heart.

2 Muscular organ which pumps blood around the body.

**ACROSS**

3 Blood vessels that carry blood back to the heart.

4 The upper chambers of the heart.

5 Blood vessels that connect the veins and arteries.

6 Blood vessels that carry blood from the heart to the rest of the body.

## 7 Order the stages of circulation.

**a** Deoxygenated blood enters the heart through the right atrium.

**b** From here, the blood is pumped around the body through the arteries.

**c** In the lungs, the blood passes through the alveoli and picks up oxygen and gets rid of carbon dioxide.

**d** The blood then passes to the right ventricle, where it is pumped into the lungs.

**e** The oxygenated blood is then pumped into the left atrium and passes into the left ventricle.

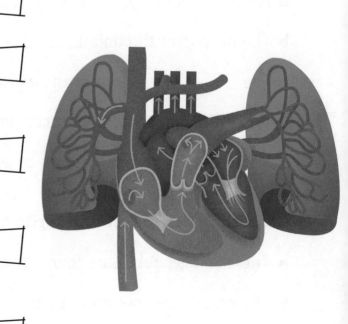

**8 Write the words in the correct order to make sentences.**

**a** diaphragm / the / is / The / lungs. / below

_____

**b** The / human / is / the / heart / of / pump / body. / the

_____

**c** 1200 / nine-year-old / child / A / breaths / hour. / takes / per

_____

**d** system. / Blood / like / a / is / delivery

_____

**e** lungs / The / are / for / responsible / breathing.

_____

**9 Cross out the incorrect word or words in each sentence and write the correct word(s) on the line.**

**a** Oxygen goes in, carbon dioxide comes in. _____

**b** The blood in the veins is rich in oxygen. _____

**c** Oxygenated blood is pumped into the right atrium. _____

**d** Carbon dioxide leaves the blood through the atrium. _____

**e** Blood carries oxygen, water and nutrients from all the cells in the human body. _____

5

**10** **Read the sentences and decide whether they describe the *respiratory system* or the *circulatory system* or *both*.**

**a** Oxygen passes from the alveoli into the blood. _____

**b** Oxygenated blood is pumped around the body. _____

**c** Carbon dioxide leaves the body through the mouth and nose. _____

**d** Carbon dioxide leaves the blood through the alveoli. _____

**e** Air enters the body through the mouth and nose. _____

**11** **Circle the parts of the respiratory system in blue and the parts of the circulatory system in red. Circle the parts that belong to both in purple.**

tracheaarterycapillarybronchilung

veinalveoliheartdiaphragm

**12** **Order the stages of breathing using ordinal numbers. There is one example.**

**a** Air enters the alveoli. _____fifth_____

**b** Air passes into the blood. _____

**c** Air passes through the bronchi. _____

**d** Air enters the nose and mouth. _____

**e** Air passes through the bronchioles. _____

**f** Air passes through the trachea. _____

**13** Angelina is talking to her mother, who has some news to tell her. Angelina is asking a lot of questions.

Read the conversation and choose the best answer. Write a number (1–8) for each answer. There is one example.

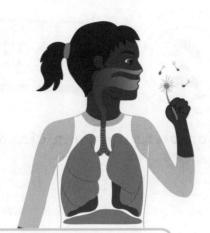

**Example**

>  **Angelina:** Mum, what is the news you want to tell me?
>
> **Mother:** _____8_____

**Questions**

a  **Angelina:** Why?

 **Mother:** _____

b  **Angelina:** How do I take it?

 **Mother:** _____

c  **Angelina:** When should I take it?

 **Mother:** _____

d  **Angelina:** Do I have to use it for a long time?

 **Mother:** _____

e **Angelina:** Can my friends use it?

**Mother:** _____

**Answer box**

1 No, they can't. It's only for you to use.
2 The medicine is in a bottle. You must breathe it in.
3 Perhaps for a few weeks.
4 Yes, you can run around with your friends more.
5 Because the doctor says you have an illness called asthma.
6 It's called an inhaler.
7 In the morning and at night.
8 I picked up your new medicine at the chemist's today.

 **2** **HOW ARE YOU FEELING?**

**1 Complete the Venn diagram.**

> sore throat   low fever   symptoms start slowly   blocked nose
> high fever   sneezing   strong body aches   coughing
> mild body aches   symptoms start quickly

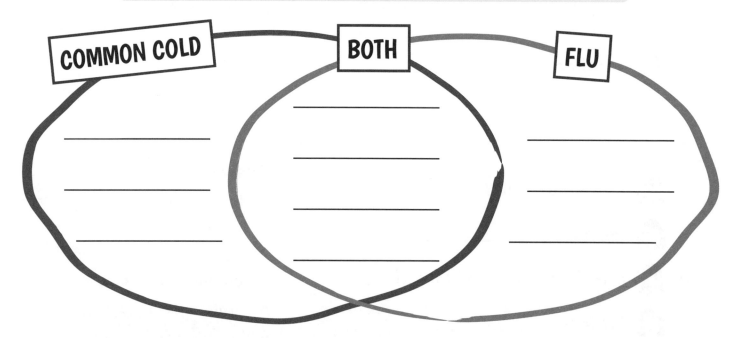

COMMON COLD

BOTH

FLU

_____

_____

_____

_____

_____

_____

_____

_____

_____

_____

**2 Complete the sentences using the words in the box.**

> chicken pox   common cold   influenza
> respiratory system   stronger

**a** The common cold affects the upper _____ .

**b** There is no vaccine for the _____ .

**c** The flu is a shorter name for _____ .

**d** The flu is a _____ illness than the common cold.

**e** The main symptom of _____ is a rash.

# 3 Identify the injuries and medical problems and what first aid should be given to each person.

Cover it and apply pressure.    Keep them still and support the injury.

Put it under cold running water.    Someone has a broken bone.

Someone has a big cut.    Someone has burnt their finger.

# 4 Match to make correct sentences.

**a** People who suffer from asthma ○          ○    call emergency services and try to get the help of an adult.

**b** First aid is help we give to someone ○          ○ we need to take medicine to get better.

**c** Sometimes, when we are ill ○          ○ use an inhaler.

**d** If you think an injury is serious, ○          ○ when they are not near a doctor or hospital.

**5 Match the foods to the nutrients they are rich in.**

 **a** Apples, oranges and pears ○ ○ Protein and iron

 **b** Beef, chicken and fish ○ ○ Carbohydrates

 **c** Milk, yoghurt and cheese ○ ○ Fats

**d** Olive oil, nuts and avocadoes ○ ○ Vitamins and minerals

 **e** Bread, pasta and rice ○ ○ Calcium

**6 Complete the sentences with *should* or *shouldn't*.**

**a** You _____ spend lots of time in front of screens.

**b** You _____ brush your teeth after every meal.

**c** You _____ eat fast food every day.

**d** You _____ have showers frequently.

**e** You _____ use a tissue when you blow your nose.

**f** You _____ stay up past your bed time.

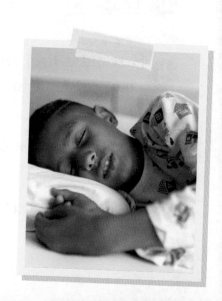

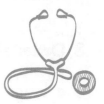

**7 Identify the medical tests in the pictures and the parts of the body or body systems they check up on. There is one example.**

Test: *The doctor is checking his mouth and throat*

Body part / system:

*Respiratory and digestive systems*

Test: _____

_____

_____

Body part / system:

_____

_____

Test: _____

_____

_____

Body part / system:

_____

_____

Test: _____

_____

_____

Body part / system:

_____

_____

Test: _____

_____

_____

Body part / system:

_____

_____

**8 Order the words to make sentences.**

**a** lungs. / can / damage / Tobacco / your

_____

**b** to / It / avoid / important / is / habits. / unhealthy

_____

**c** Being / can / around / mind / people / positive / your / keep / healthy.

_____

**d** avoid / eating / should / lots / salt. / food / with / of / We

_____

**9 Look at the three pictures. Write about this story.
Write 20 or more words.**

_____

_____

_____

_____

**10 Read the diary and write the missing words. Write one word on each line.**

For the last two weeks, we have learnt about healthy __habits__ in natural science class. I'm really enjoying the topic and I'm learning lots of new things. I know I follow a **(a)** _____ diet but Mum is always telling me to eat more fruits and vegetables, and to drink lots of milk to get **(b)** _____ . I was worried that I wasn't getting enough **(c)** _____ because I don't really like sports, but my teacher told me that I get plenty of exercise from my karate **(d)** _____ . I do need to change one habit. I think I **(e)** _____ too much time playing games on my tablet. My **(f)** _____ need a rest, too!

## 3 IS A SPONGE AN ANIMAL?

**1 Decide whether the animals are *vertebrates* or *invertebrates*.**

a _____

b _____

c _____

d _____

e _____

**2 Write sentences about how these animals breathe.**

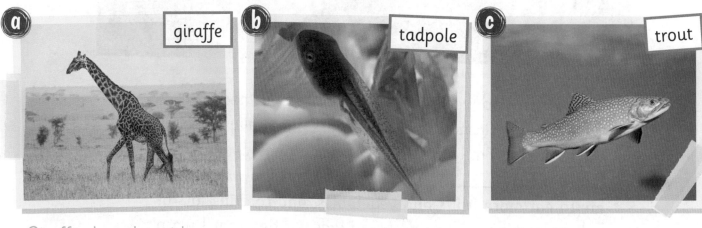

a giraffe

b tadpole

c trout

Giraffes breathe with
their lungs.

_____

_____

_____

_____

d frog

e rhinoceros

_____

_____

_____

_____

**3 Use the words and the pictures to write sentences about bird nutrition.**

**a** cone-shaped beaks

sparrow

**b** long, pointed beaks

heron

**c** long, thick beaks

toucan

**d** long, strong beaks

woodpecker

**e** hooked beaks

hawk

**f** long, thick beaks

hummingbird

**a** Sparrows have cone-shaped beaks for eating seeds.

**b** _____

**c** _____

**d** _____

**e** _____

**f** _____

**4 Order the stages of metamorphosis from 1–5.**

**a** A tadpole emerges from each egg.

**b** Finally, it leaves the water.

**c** An adult female frog lays her eggs in the water.

**d** Its legs get stronger and its tail reduces in size.

**e** The tadpole develops back and front legs.

**5 Match to make true sentences about respiration.**

a Adult amphibians ○

b Birds ○

c Fish ○

d Mammals ○

e Reptiles ○

f Young amphibians ○

○ breathe using lungs.

○ breathe using gills.

○ breathe through their skin.

**6 Look and read. Choose the correct words and write them on the lines. There is one example.**

amphibians

caterpillar

eagle

filament

hatch

iguana

a These mammals lay eggs. _monotremes_

b These birds have long, thick beaks for eating fruit. _____

c Most birds build these things to protect their eggs from predators. _____

d This is what we call it when birds sit on their eggs to keep them warm. _____

e This is what we call it when a chick breaks through its egg. _____

f This reptile is a herbivore. _____

g Members of this vertebrate group have a long, sticky tongue. _____

h This part of a fish's gills absorbs oxygen. _____

incubate

jaws

~~monotremes~~

nests

oviparous

toucans

**7 Find the six main invertebrate groups in the wordsearch.**

| X | K | J | N | C | Y | W | W | Z | E | R |
|---|---|---|---|---|---|---|---|---|---|---|
| A | S | E | A | N | V | Y | R | Z | C | P |
| N | R | B | K | I | E | E | M | E | H | O |
| N | N | T | B | D | O | N | L | M | I | R |
| E | Y | Y | H | A | R | J | Z | U | N | I |
| L | C | L | Z | R | W | H | F | X | O | F |
| I | H | T | P | I | O | G | X | A | D | E |
| D | X | V | G | A | R | P | J | F | E | R |
| S | P | O | Q | N | N | F | O | Y | R | A |
| T | E | I | R | S | L | U | G | D | M | N |
| C | Z | M | O | L | L | U | S | C | S | S |

**8 Classify the arthropod characteristics below. You may use some words twice.**

largest group   ten legs   eight legs   no antennae
front legs are claws   no wings   one pair of antennae
six legs   some have wings   three body sections
two body sections   two pairs of antennae

| Insects | Crustaceans | Arachnids |
|---|---|---|
| largest group | | |
| | | |
| | | |
| | | |
| | | |

**9** **Write ticks to complete the table.**

|  | Abdomen | Head | Thorax | Cephalothorax |
|---|---|---|---|---|
| **Crustaceans** | ✓ |  |  |  |
| **Arachnids** |  |  |  |  |
| **Insects** |  |  |  |  |

**10** **Use the words in the box to complete the sentences.**

> foot　head　internal　rings　shell　valves

**a** Almost all molluscs have a _____ .

**b** Gastropods have a large muscular _____ that helps them move.

**c** Cephalopods have an _____ shell and a prominent _____ .

**d** The shell of a bivalve is divided into two _____ .

**e** An annelid's body is long and soft, and made up of _____ .

**11** **Complete the crossword using words from the unit.**

**ACROSS**

**1** The name of this invertebrate means 'prickly skin'.

**4** Sponges have these on their body. Water passes through them.

**5** This cnidarian sometimes stings people swimming in the sea.

**6** These invertebrates have venomous tentacles.

**DOWN**

**2** This is the type of shell a cephalopod has.

**3** This is another name for a sponge.

**12** Jonathan is talking to his uncle Paul, who is an entomologist. Jonathan is studying arthropods and has some questions.

Read the conversation and choose the best answers.
Write a number (1–8) for each answer. There is one example.

**Example**

>  **Jonathan:** What do entomologists do?
>
>  **Paul:** _____ 8 _____

**Questions**

**a**  **Jonathan:** So, you only know about insects?

    **Paul:** _____

**b** **Jonathan:** Oh good! You can help me. I have some questions.

   **Paul:** _____

**c**  **Jonathan:** My teacher says spiders are not insects. Is it true?

   **Paul:** _____

**d**  **Jonathan:** But look at these pictures. Their bodies look so similar!

   **Paul:** _____

**e**  **Jonathan:** Wow, you're right. But their legs are the same.

    **Paul:** _____

**Answer box**

1 That's right, they are arachnids.

2 Molluscs have tentacles, not antennae.

3 Insects are my speciality, but I know a lot about other invertebrates as well.

4 No, they aren't. Arachnids have eight, but insects only have six.

5 Most crustaceans live in the water.

6 Ask me whatever you want.

7 Look more closely. Arachnids have two body sections, but insects have three.

8 Entomologists study insects.

**1 Read the sentences and decide if they describe *sexual reproduction* (SR) or *asexual reproduction* (AR) in plants.**

**a** Male and female parts are involved in this type of reproduction. _____

**b** Male and female parts are not involved in this type of reproduction. _____

**c** Fertilisation takes place. _____

**d** A new plant does not grow from a seed. _____

**e** A new plant grows from a seed. _____

**f** Fertilisation does not take place. _____

**2 Label the diagram of the flower.**

| petal ~~stamen~~ anther filament pollen pistil stigma style ovule ovary sepals |
|---|

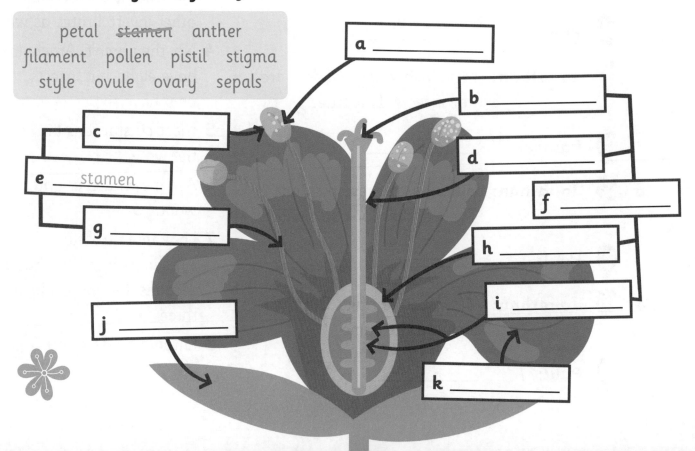

a _____

b _____

c _____

d _____

e ___stamen___

f _____

g _____

h _____

i _____

j _____

k _____

**3** Classify the words in the box as parts of the male or female reproductive organs.

> anther   filament   ovary   pistil   pollen   ovule
> stamen   stigma   style

| Male reproductive organs | Female reproductive organs |
| --- | --- |
|  |  |
|  |  |
|  |  |
|  |  |
|  |  |

**4** Explain the function of these parts of the flower.

**a** The ovary _contains the ovules, which are the female cells._

**b** The anther _____

**c** The ovules _____

**d** The petals _____

**e** The sepals _____

**f** The stigma _____

**g** The style _____

**5 Match to make true sentences.**

**a** Rhizomes ○

**b** Stolons ○

**c** Tubers ○

○ are also called runners.

○ are like thick stems which grow underground.

○ grow horizontally along the ground.

○ can be eaten, for example the potato.

○ grow horizontally underground.

**6 Complete the photosynthesis formula.**

water + _____ + _____   solar energy → _____ + oxygen

**7 Order the steps of animal pollination.**

**a** Some of the pollen gets stuck on the stigma of the pistil.

**b** The fertilised ovule develops into a seed.

**c** Insects and small birds pick up pollen from a flower.

**d** The seed falls to the ground and a new plant begins to grow.

**e** They get covered in pollen while feeding on nectar.

**f** They transport the pollen from the stamen to the pistil of the same plant or other plants.

**g** When the flower withers and dies, the seeds are spread.

**h** Some of the pollen travels down to the ovary and fertilises the ovules.

1

**8 Look and read. Choose the correct words and write them on the lines. There is one example.**

anther

asexually

carbon dioxide

chlorophyll

filament

glucose

leaves

**a** This part of the plant absorbs water and nutrients from the soil. _____roots_____

**b** The water and nutrients are transported up this part of the plant. _____

**c** These are the tubes through which water and nutrients travel. _____

**d** These are the tiny pores on the leaves. _____

**e** The tiny pores on the leaves absorb this substance from the air. _____

**f** This is the green substance plants use to absorb solar energy. _____

**g** This is the food the plant produces during photosynthesis. _____

**h** This is the gas that is produced during photosynthesis. _____

**i** The plant's food is transported around the plant through these tubes. _____

oxygen

phloem

~~roots~~

sexually

stem

stomata

xylem

**9** Label the diagram of plant respiration with the words *carbon dioxide* and *oxygen*.

a _____

b _____

c _____

d _____

e _____

**10 Complete the crossword using words from the unit.**

**DOWN**

**1** Plants make their own food, so they are ...

**2** The release of this gas into the atmosphere contributes to global warming.

**4** Mosses and ferns reproduce using these reproductive cells.

**ACROSS**

**3** Some animals live in or around plants. This is the animal's ...

**5** Fruits and vegetables give us ... and energy.

**6** By planting more of these, we can help reduce global warming.

**11 Read the story. Choose a word from the box. Write the correct word next to letters a–e. There is one example.**

plants  asexually  global warming  nutrition  tubers
photosynthesis  respiration  rhizomes  sexually  stolons

Fiona is in year 4 of primary school. She is passionate about nature. She is particularly interested in animals. This week, her class has been learning about ____plants____ . She is fascinated by **(a)** _____ , the process by which plants make their own food. She did not realise just how important plants are for all living things. They produce oxygen, which all living things need to perform **(b)** _____ . They also provide food for us to eat. Fiona was surprised to learn that potatoes are **(c)** _____ . These are like thick stems which grow under the ground. This type of plant reproduces **(d)** _____ .

Fiona wants her mother to help her do something. 'Mum, can we plant a tree?' asks Fiona. 'Of course we can!' replies her mother. 'But why do you want to plant a tree?' asks her mother. 'Because it helps reduce the effects of **(e)** _____ . And maybe some animals will make it their home!'

# 5 WHICH FORCES ARE INVISIBLE?

**1 Read the sentences and decide if they refer to *mass* or *volume*.**

**a** This is the amount of space an object occupies. _____

**b** This is measured in grams and kilograms. _____

**c** We measure this with a weighing scales. _____

**d** We measure this with a measuring jug. _____

**e** We measure this in litres and millilitres. _____

**f** This is the amount of matter in an object. _____

**2 Look at the pictures below. Determine the volume of the object.**

The volume of the object is _____ .

**3 Look at the pictures. Write which state of matter you can see in each one.**

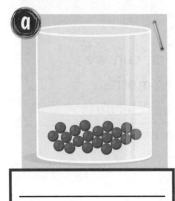

_____

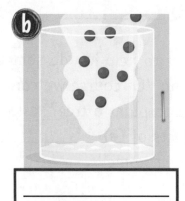

_____

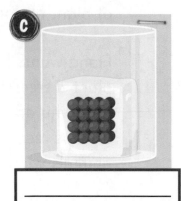

_____

# 4 Look at the pictures. Write which process you can see in each one.

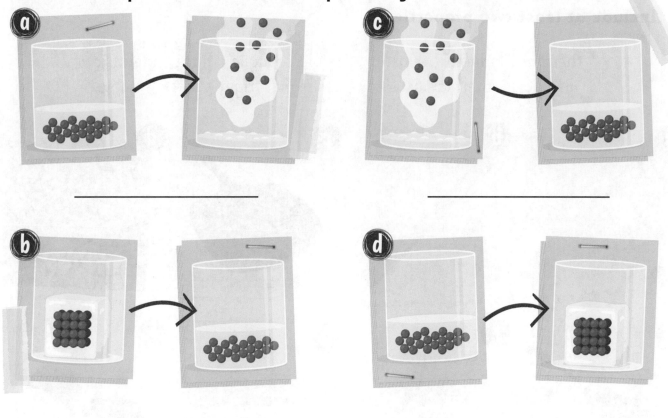

**a** _____

**c** _____

**b** _____

**d** _____

# 5 Complete the sentences. Two words must be used twice.

> materials   matter   properties   states

**a** Matter occurs in three different _____ : solid, liquid and gas.

**b** _____ are substances which are made up of matter.

**c** Materials can be made of one type of _____ or more than one type of _____ .

**d** Depending on their _____ , we use different _____ to make different things.

**6 Write sentences to describe the properties of these objects.**
**Include at least two properties.**

| thermal conductor | elastic | flexible | fragile | hard | inelastic |
| insoluble | thermal insulator | resistant | rigid | soft | soluble |

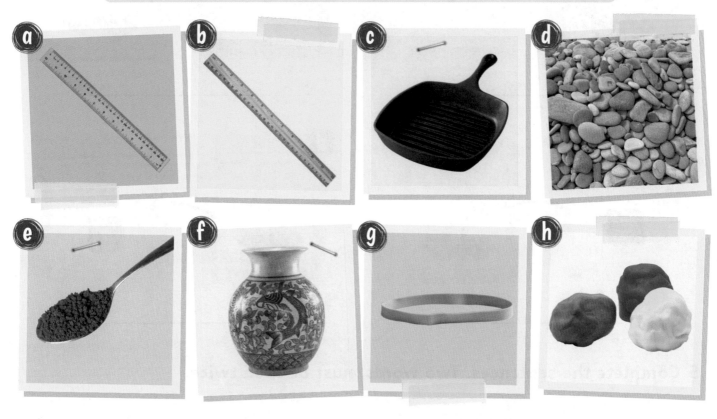

a    The plastic ruler is hard, flexible and resistant. It is also a thermal insulator.

b _____

c _____

d _____

e _____

f _____

g _____

h _____

**7 Complete the crossword with words from the unit.**

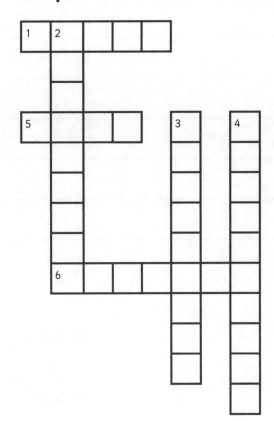

### DOWN

**2** This word describes materials which do not dissolve in liquids.

**3** This word describes materials that are hard to break.

**4** This word describes materials through which heat passes easily.

### ACROSS

**1** This word describes materials which are difficult to bend.

**5** This word describes materials which are easy to scratch.

**6** This word describes material which are easy to stretch.

**8 Do these sentences describe *contact* forces, *non-contact* forces or *both*?**

**a** The needle of a compass points north.  _____

**b** You make a ball out of a sheet of paper.  _____

**c** You open your book.  _____

**d** You knock your pencil case off your desk and it falls to the ground.  _____

9 Write examples of the following forces.

a **Push:** When you open a door.

b **Pull:** _____

c **Friction:** _____

d **Gravity:** _____

e **Magnetism:** _____

f **Change shape:** _____

10 **Match.**

Light for its size ○                                    ○ High density

                                                       ○ Low density

Heavy for its size ○                                   ○ It floats in liquid.

                                                       ○ It sinks in liquid.

11 **Label the picture, then complete the text.**

When you place an object in water, **(a)** _____ pushes the object
**(b)** _____ , and **(c)** _____ pushes the object **(d)** _____ .

**12 Read the story. Write some words to complete the sentences about the story. You can use 1, 2, 3 or 4 words.**

## Cillian's family go shopping

Cillian is growing up very quickly. He is getting taller and taller every day. His mother thinks his bed is too small for him, so his family go shopping for a new one. On Saturday morning, they go to a department store.

Cillian's father really likes cooking. He wants to buy some things for the kitchen, so first they go to the kitchen department. 'That metal spoon I use for cooking stew is no good! I want to buy a plastic one!' says Cillian's dad.

'Why do you want a plastic one, Dad?' asks Cillian's sister, Orla. 'Plastic is a thermal insulator,' explains Cillian's dad. 'That means the heat from the soup doesn't pass easily to the spoon and burn Dad's hand!' says Cillian. 'I know what a thermal insulator is!' replies Orla. 'Oh really? Do you know what a thermal conductor is?' asks Cillian. 'Of course, I do! The metal in that frying pan is a thermal conductor. And the handle is plastic, so you don't burn your hand,' replies Orla. 'That's enough, you two,' says Cillian's mother. 'Let's go look at the beds.'

Cillian lies down on a bed to see if it is comfortable. 'This one is too hard,' he says. 'Try this one,' says his dad. 'This one is a bit softer, but it's not too soft.' 'And it has a metal frame. Metal is less fragile than wood,' says Cillian's mother. 'And I know how you like jumping on your bed! Let's get it.'

**a** Cillian's dad wants to buy a _____ cooking spoon.

**b** Cillian's dad wants a plastic spoon because it is a thermal _____ .

**c** The metal spoon is no good because metal is a thermal _____ .

**d** The frying pan Orla and Cillian argue about has a plastic _____ because it is a thermal _____ .

**e** Cillian's mum likes the second bed because its _____ frame is less _____ than a wooden one.

31

# HOW HAVE MACHINES CHANGED THE WORLD?

**1 Classify the following machines as *simple* or *complex* machines.**

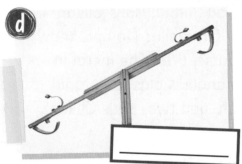

**2 Complete the sentences.**

**a** Simple machines have few or no _____ parts.

**b** Complex machines have _____ parts and contain _____ machines.

**c** A _____ is the weight of an object.

**d** Effort is the amount of _____ required to lift the load.

**3 Look at these two ramps. Which one requires less effort? Why? Write a full answer.**

_____

_____

_____

_____

**4 Read the descriptions and decide whether they refer to an *inclined plane*, a *pulley* or *both*.**

**a** This simple machine consists of a wheel and a rope or cable. _____

**b** When you pull one end of the rope, the other end goes up. _____

**c** We use this simple machine to move heavy loads up and down. _____

**d** We have to apply effort to make this simple machine work. _____

**e** The smaller the incline, the easier it is to move the load up. _____

**f** This simple machine has a surface which goes from a low point to a high point. _____

**5 Label the diagram of a pulley.**

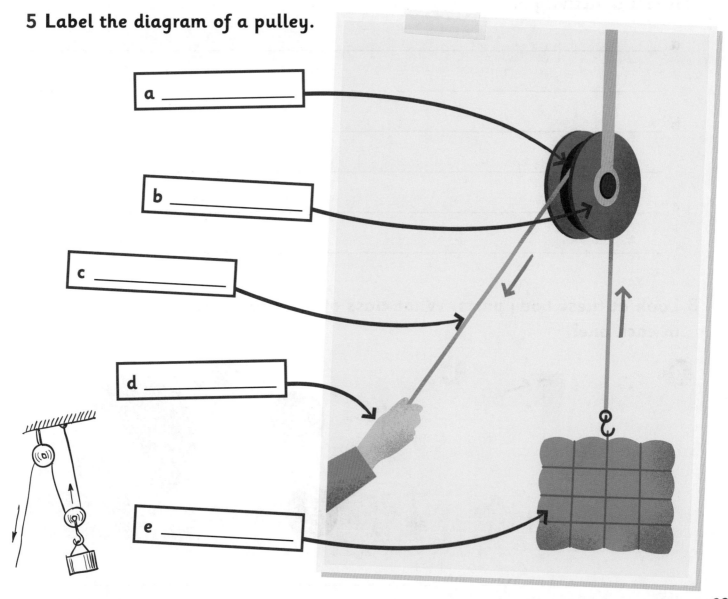

a _____

b _____

c _____

d _____

e _____

**6 Look at the pictures and decide which class of lever you can see in each one.**

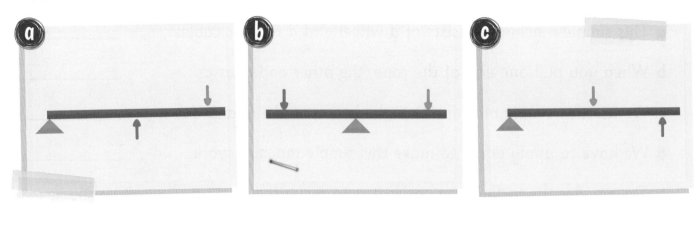

_____     _____     _____

**7 Describe the relationship between the load, effort and fulcrum in the levers in activity 6.**

a _____

_____

b _____

_____

c _____

_____

**8 Look at these body parts. What class of lever can you see in each one?**

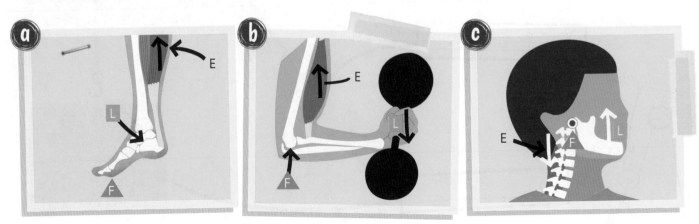

_____     _____     _____

## 9 Identify the class of each of these levers.

_____

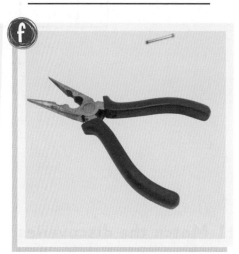

_____

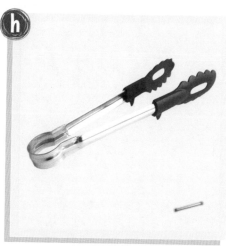

_____

## 10 Complete the crossword.

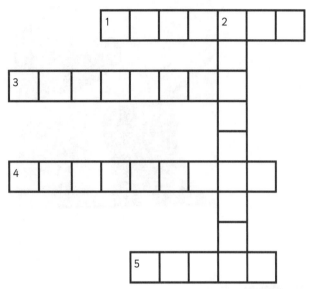

### ACROSS

**1** Before this was invented, navigators had to use landmarks to find their way.

**3** This invention allowed people to prepare documents and play games in their homes.

**4** Before this was invented, people had to use oil lamps or candles to illuminate their homes.

**5** Before this was invented, people had to push or pull loads along the ground.

### DOWN

**2** Before this was invented, international travel took a long time.

## 11 Match the discoveries to the dates.

**a** The compass ○                    ○ AD 1974

**b** The personal computer ○          ○ 200 BC

**c** The light bulb ○                  ○ AD 1903

**d** The aeroplane ○                   ○ 3500 BC

**e** The wheel ○                       ○ AD 1879

## 12 Read the text. Choose the right words and write them on the lines.

### Archimedes of Syracuse

Archimedes was an ___Ancient___ Greek mathematician and engineer. He was born in 287 BC in the city of Syracuse, **(a)** _____ the Island of Sicily, which today forms part **(b)** _____ Italy. When he was 10 years old, he **(c)** _____ Syracuse to study in Alexandria, in Ancient Egypt. When he returned, he **(d)** _____ working for the King of Syracuse. One day, the King asked Archimedes to help him **(e)** _____ a problem. A gold crown had been made for him, and he wanted to make sure that it was **(f)** _____ made out of gold. There was one condition: Archimedes **(g)** _____ damage the crown. While having a bath, Archimedes realised that he **(h)** _____ calculate the density of an object by dividing its mass by its volume. He was so excited, that he jumped from his bath and **(i)** _____ down the city streets shouting 'eureka!', which **(j)** _____ 'I have found it!'.

EUREKA!

| Example | Modern | Present | ~~Ancient~~ |
|---|---|---|---|
| **a** | in | on | at |
| **b** | of | in | with |
| **c** | left | leaves | will leave |
| **d** | began | stopped | finished |
| **e** | on | at | with |
| **f** | complete | completely | completing |
| **g** | could not | might not | cannot |
| **h** | will be able | might | could |
| **i** | run | ran | will run |
| **j** | means | mean | does not mean |

Try writing these words in your own language!

## Unit 1
### How do our body systems work?

alveoli (n) _____

artery (n) _____

atrium (n) _____

blood (n) _____

blood vessel (n) _____

body system (n) _____

breathing (n) _____

bronchi (n) _____

bronchiole (n) _____

capillary (n) _____

carbon dioxide (n) _____

circulation (n) _____

contract (v) _____

diaphragm (n) _____

lung capacity (n) _____

measure (v) _____

organ (n) _____

oxygen (n) _____

relax (v) _____

respiration (n) _____

trachea (n) _____

urethra (n) _____

valve (n) _____

vein (n) _____

ventricle (n) _____

vital (adj) _____

## Unit 2
### How are you feeling?

check-up (n) _____

chicken pox (n) _____

common cold (n) _____

contagious (adj) _____

contaminate (v) _____

cough (v) _____

fall ill (v) _____

fast food (n) _____

fever (n) _____

first aid (n) _____

flu (n) _____

function (v) _____

have a runny nose (phr) _____

illness (n) _____

improve (v) _____

injured (adj) _____

injury (n) _____

measure (v) _____

personal hygiene (n) _____

rash (n) _____

recover (v) _____

sneezing (n) _____

sphygmomanometer (n) _____

stethoscope (n) _____

support (v) _____

tissue (n) _____

vaccine (n) _____

## Unit 3
## Is a sponge an animal?

air sac (n) _____

appendage (n) _____

attach (v) _____

beak (n) _____

blowhole (n) _____

carnivore (n) _____

cephalothorax (n) _____

claw (n) _____

emerge (v) _____

expel (v) _____

filament (n) _____

gills (n) _____

herbivore (n) _____

hold your breath (phr) _____

hooked (adj) _____

incubate (v) _____

invertebrate (n) _____

lungs (n) _____

monotreme (n) _____

omnivore (n) _____

pointed (adj) _____

prickly (adj) _____

segmented (adj) _____

tentacle (n) _____

thorax (n) _____

venom (n) _____

vertebrate (n) _____

## Unit 4
## Why are plants so important?

anther (n) _____

asexually (adv) _____

chlorophyll (n) _____

climate change (n) _____

fertilise (v) _____

filament (n) _____

global warming (n) _____

glucose (n) _____

habitat (n) _____

nectar (n) _____

ovary (n) _____

ovule (n) _____

petal (n) _____

phloem (n) _____

pick up (v) _____

pistil (n) _____

pollen (n) _____

rhizome (n) _____

sepal (n) _____

sexually (adv) _____

stamen (n) _____

stigma (n) _____

stolon (n) _____

stomata (n) _____

style (n) _____

tuber (n) _____

xylem (n) _____

## Unit 5
### Which forces are invisible?

atom (n) _____

attract (v) _____

buoyancy (n) _____

condense (v) _____

conductor (n) _____

density (n) _____

elastic (adj) _____

evaporate (v) _____

friction (n) _____

gram (n) _____

gravity (n) _____

inelastic (adj) _____

insoluble (adj) _____

insulator (n) _____

kilogram (n) _____

magnetism (n) _____

mass (n) _____

matter (n) _____

melt (v) _____

mould (v) _____

occupy (v) _____

property (n) _____

repel (v) _____

rubber (n) _____

solidify (v) _____

soluble (adj) _____

volume (n) _____

## Unit 6
### How have inventions changed the world?

bottle opener (n) _____

cable (n) _____

capsize (v) _____

effort (n) _____

engineer (n) _____

fulcrum (n) _____

heavy (adj) _____

hollow (adj) _____

hook (n) _____

invent (v) _____

lever (n) _____

load (n) _____

low-lying (adj) _____

motion (n) _____

nutcracker (n) _____

oar (n) _____

pliers (n) _____

ruler (n) _____

see-saw (n) _____

sink (v) _____

stapler (n) _____

tilted (adj) _____

tongs (n) _____

tweezers (n) _____

wheelbarrow (n) _____

windmill (n) _____